Tell the Truth
& SHAME THE DEVIL:

Accepting Your Truth to Reclaim Your

POWER

Tell the Truth & SHAME THE DEVIL:

Accepting Your Truth to Reclaim Your

POWER

DR. S. COLLINS

Copyright © 2018, Dr. S. Collins. All rights reserved. No part of this book may be reproduced or transmitted in any form or by any means, electronic or mechanical, including photocopying, recording, or by any information storage or retrieval system, without permission in writing from the author.

Layout and design by
Idea to Profit, Dallas, TX.
1910 Pacific Ave Suite 14180
Dallas, TX 75201
www.ideatoprofit.co

Manuscript Critique Service by
Ink Pen Diva
www.inkpendiva.com

To order please contact:
dfdentistry@yahoo.com

Printed through Ingram Spark.

Printed in the United States of America.

All photos, concepts, instructions, and other materials in this book belong to Dr. S. Collins.

All rights reserved.

ISBN 13: 978-0-692-09485-3

Dedication

To my brother, gone, but never forgotten. I love you. Until we meet again…

Acknowledgements

Thank you to my children for your unwavering love. To my mom and dad, thank you! I would not be who I am today without your ongoing prayers. And to my wife, thank you for your patience and being my anchor. Through it all, you have been an intricate contributor to my development as a husband, father, and most importantly, as an imperfect man witnessing for God.

Thank you to my Lord and Savior Jesus Christ through whom all things are possible and able. Thank you for your mercy and grace, which continue to follow me all the days of my life.

Chapters

Dedication	xv
Acknowledgements	xvii
Foreword	xiii
Addiction Can Happen to Anyone	1
Introduction	1
Choosing Dentistry	27
Becoming a C- Alcoholic	34
The Addict's Alphabet	43
Surrendering to the Lord	59
Values	63
Dealing with Self (Self- Control)	69
Lessons and Tools	81
About the Author	95

"Your Life as a believer should make non-believers doubt their disbelief in God."

~Dietrich Bonhoeffer

Foreword

When I received a call requesting that I write the foreword for this book, I was quite honored that my background, experience, and credentials qualified Dr. Collins' to ask me to be a part of his first book. Before I agreed, I needed to read the book and then I would need to meet and talk to Dr. Collins. I received the book, and right away the title jumped out at me. I said to myself, "This is either a great book or a great hype job." The latter was something I did not want to be a part of. Intriguingly, in my research of Dr. Collins, I found out that he was not an apostle, bishop, pastor, minister, counselor, or therapist as I am; but a dentist. I said to myself, "Andrew, you have the book and signed the Non-Disclosure agreement. Read the book!"

I read it, twice, and I enjoyed it! I could relate to his struggle of the human condition. I appreciated his manuscript, a compelling story of God's grace and receiving the salvation of Jesus Christ. I was excited and could not wait to speak to Dr. Collins. When we finally connected, we talked for two and a half hours.

Dr. Collins made me feel like he was shouting to the world that, at any given moment, he had the power to say that no matter how bad things were in his life, he was determined that his story was not going to end the same way! He truly understands that, with God on his side, losing his soul or his family was not an option.

I have been given the distinct opportunity and honor to introduce you to a man of God that has the courage to share his achievements, his perils, his failures, his faults, and at times, his lack of faith. He fell and realized that with all his success, he was missing God in his life. Dr. Collins grasped onto John 3:16 and found Jesus.

"For God so loved the world, that he gave his only begotten Son, that whosoever believeth in him should not perish, but have everlasting life."
John 3:16 KJV

Tell the Truth and Shame the Devil will show you the power of God's love, evident in the author's life. Dr. Collins' new relationship with God has allowed him to be defined, not by his failures, but by his triumph and his ability to live an II Corinthians 5:17-18 lifestyle.

> **"Therefore, if any man be in Christ, he is a new creature: old things are passed away; behold, all things are become new. And all things are of God, who hath reconciled us to himself by Jesus Christ, and hath given to us the ministry of reconciliation;"**
> **II Cor 5:17-18 KJV**

Dr. Collins poignantly shares his past sins as examples of what not to do. As you turn the page, read with your faith eyes and not with judgment. Tell the Truth and Shame the Devil addresses the issues of life from a true testimonial approach. The author is begging you not to look at him as the hero of his story, but as the reformed villain that was saved by a true hero who died for our sins- Jesus.

Join me in thanking Dr. Collins for his courage to share.

Dr. Andrew Watkins Sr. Ph.D.
Licensed Biblical Therapist
Board Certified Faith Based Clinical Counselor
Anger Mgmt. Consultant & Specialist 2
Certified Behavioral Analyst
Christian Behaviorist

Preface

Addiction Can Happen to Anyone

"Don't forget me." ~ **Dr. S. Collins**

Addiction does not discriminate. Addiction comes in all forms and consumes lives, families, and careers. My addiction was rooted in isolation and infused with the environment I chose to place myself. I chose alcohol which became my addiction. The book is not exclusively about alcoholism, but how to identify the root issue and cause of your life that has led to addiction; and how to overcome the addiction God's way. It is important to understand the enemy that we are fighting and therefore I want to share some statistics about addiction and alcoholism to put us in the proper frame of mind.

According to Healthyplace.com, there are many addictions to substances that people struggle with:
- Alcohol
- Tobacco
- Opioids (e.g. heroin)
- Prescription drugs
- Cocaine

- Cannabis (marijuana)
- Amphetamines (known as meth)
- Hallucinogens
- Inhalants
- Phencyclidine (known as PCP or Angel Dust)

Addictions are not always substances. They can be self-inflicting behaviors, acts, and injuries. Others struggle with sex addiction and mental health disorders such as bipolar disorder or borderline personality disorder. Healthyplace.com estimated that about one in 10 young people who plays video games have an addiction to the behavior. Compulsive shopping is often believed to be a problem amongst women, but CNN reports that only about six percent of women struggle with the problem – and so do 5.5 percent of men.

Gambling addiction may impact up to 2-3 percent of the American public. Its signs, symptoms, and impacts may vary across genders, age groups, and other populations. Though similar, food addiction is different from binge eating disorder.

According to the National Institute on Alcohol Abuse and Alcoholism, an estimated 88,000 people (approximately 62,000 men and 26,000 women), die from alcohol-related causes annually, making alcohol the third leading preventable cause of death in the United States. The first is tobacco, and the second is poor diet and physical inactivity. In 2014, alcohol-impaired driving fatalities (DUI) accounted for 9,967 deaths (31 percent of overall driving fatalities). Three-quarters of the total cost of alcohol misuse is related to binge drinking. More than 10 percent of U.S. children live with a parent with alcohol problems, according to a 2012 study.

All in all, addiction is killing people and destroying families. This is an epidemic and we must shed light on the truth and attack the root causes behind them. I have walked this process in my own life, attempting to tell the truth, and shame the devil, to overcome my own personal addiction. I will share some truths I have learned and experiences that led to my recovery, in hopes that you too, or your friend or loved one, will do the same.

Disclaimer: This book is not a medical book meant to diagnose or treat any illness or condition. The definitions in this book are not intended to diagnose. Please consult a doctor and if this is a medical emergency, please call 911.

Introduction

Why am I writing a Tell-All book of scandal that in the deep-South, would shame a family's name? The mere fact that I am a dentist, promotes a type of undeniable hierarchy that, like a minister, encourages the masses to scrutinize and watch his behavior. Could this be, again, a reckless decision endangering my career or my family's reputation?

I am here to tell you that this assignment that I have fought for years is not of my own, but God's order for me. My desire is to share with you the many mistakes that I have made in which some would see shame, but I see as an opportunity to grow. Shame! Through the many reality shows, time and again, we have investigated the lives of others, ridiculing their faults, and yet encouraging more. We see the drug addict or stripper in the church and ask each other, "Do you see her? Why is she here?" Not understanding this is exactly where she should be. We glorify the destruction of others for our glory, and yet, we have hidden secrets in our own closet. Secrets that lead to suicide, depression, and even violence if exposed.

This book is my attempt at encouraging others to release their truth. The front cover of my book states, "Accepting Your Truth to Reclaim Your Power." As Jay Z once said in an interview, where he addressed his own indiscretions, "You can either address it or pretend until it blows up at some point." I love the story of Eminem through his movie, 8 Mile. This movie depicted a poor young-man, who grew-up in the ghetto of Detroit with aspirations of being a rapper. As he would battle with other neighboring rappers for the legitimacy of the king of rap title in that area, they used his poor conditions and being white to beat him in the challenges. It was only until he stopped being ashamed of being white in an all-black club and started to rap on his horrible conditions, that he began to win those rap battles. His opponents did not have anything else to say to win. How many people has he helped that have seen his story and realized that they could also be an Eminem in the making.

I am writing this book to help someone that may see themselves in my story. I want them to know that it is okay to make mistakes. The blessing of life is that through God's grace and mercy, you can make a mistake, but more so, that if God blesses you to wake up the following morning, you have another day to change it and you. I pray that whoever reads this will reach deep into themselves, unbury their own hidden secrets, and release the shame.

1
Growing up S. Collins

"I can do all things through Christ who strengthens me."

~ Philippians 4:13.

I was born on March 22, 1973 in Louisiana. I was an only child. We lived in an extremely close and poor neighborhood. I was known in the neighborhood as, "Streakier." Since the time I was able to walk, I loved to run throughout the neighborhood in the nude. My parents were mid 20 party goers. Back then, my parents, their friends, and family had weekly weekend fish fry parties at neighboring homes. These parties included a lot of Buffalo fish, Motown music, cheap beer/liquor, and everybody's damn kids. It was fun.

Being the only child, I loved spending the night with my mom's sister, Grace, and her four children including a son my age. All the kids loved spending the night at Madea's house, our grandmother, sleeping on the homemade pallet - sheets on the floor. The house was cold in the winters, even with the small gas heaters and stove, that stayed on for the duration of the night. You may have even seen a roach or a mouse; nevertheless, that was the place to be.

Madea was nothing to play with, but she loved her children and grandchildren. When my mother would spank me, I would call my grandmother to tell on her. During one particular beating, my mother, who did not play, told me that if I called Madea after this spanking, she would spank me again. I tried her and called my grandmother. My mother picked up the phone, spoke, hung up the phone, and immediately whipped my butt again. This was the beginning of me disobeying authority and trying things my way.

From the time that I could talk, I called my mother by her first name, Alma. My dad's mom, Grandmother D, expressed her concerns and displeasing thoughts about me disrespecting my mother by calling her by her first name. My mother told me that I would not and could not ever call her Alma again. So, I decided not to call her for anything, for weeks. It was only until I needed that, "must have" Hulk set that my cousin had. I then humbled myself and asked, "Momma, please, can I have it?"

My parents and I moved from that neighborhood to a more promising, but still poor neighborhood. The houses had just been bricked. Life seemed great. We continually had our fish fry parties, we were traveling to Dallas and Chicago throughout the year, and just having a great time. But around eight years old, things seemed to take a turn for the worse. There were less "old" faces at the fish fry parties. The Baby Boomers were getting divorced. My aunts and my mom's friends were calling their husbands whoremongers or worse. My parents began to argue more and fight. My happy home turned into divorce court, visitation on the weekend with my father, and soon after, a new daddy, named Willie.

My mother and Willie married when I was around nine. "Who in the hell is this man?" I wondered. He was very light-skinned as my mom, and I looked as though I did not belong because I am dark skinned. Both parents were moving on with their new relationships. A 13-year-old neighbor began to fondle me around this time. And I in turn began to fondle her. I was 10. This continued for about one year until my parents decided to move.

My new family decided to move to this low middle-class neighborhood when I was 11. I tested into a Magnet school. I started Judo and fought in a lot of tournaments that I won. Times were great again. My dad was at each tournament videoing every fight. He was proud. I was extremely popular in the sixth grade especially with the eighth graders. My eighth-grade year, I was awarded the title King of Mardi Gras. I remembered feeling attractive, because throughout my childhood, I was teased by my cousins for being too dark.

I felt extremely cool in middle school. I had the fashionable clothes, the cool Spree scooter, I was dating the hottest eighth grader, and was kicking butt in Judo. This high of admiration lasted until the middle of my seventh-grade year. One day, the phone rang, and my nosey mom answered. The young lady politely asked for me and my mother asked her, her name. She responded, "Sharika." She also asked the girl who her father was. Sharika responded, "Raymond Curtis." My mother immediately recognized the name and kindly hung up. She hurried and called Raymond and told him there was a problem. This "problem" was a secret that would change my life. My mother sat me down and stated that there was something she needed to confess. She told me that my dad, whom I have always known to be my dad, was not my biological father. My biological father was Sharika's dad. I was the victim of an adulterous affair. My father, according to my mother, had many outside relationships, which finally led her to seek attention elsewhere, and for one night, she did just that. During that same time, my parents were having child support issues. My dad was not paying his $150.00 a month properly. My mother told him to either pay or give up his parental rights. Drinking at the time, he made the biggest mistake ever and gave up his rights. However, as he was giving up his rights, Willie, my mom's husband, adopted me the same day and my last name changed. I was also told I could no longer see my Dad anymore. This is when my mother made her first huge mistake of many as a parent. By not talking me through everything that was happening and allowing me to express my anger, sadness, and confusion over this major change, I did not truly deal with it. I held everything in, there was no one to talk to. This traumatic change in my life, and the way that it was handled by the adults in charge, contributed to my issues with isolation. It further led me into a pattern in my adult life where I was not able to be truthful of my issues, sooner, for fear of hurting someone else, or being chastised for bringing it up. At a very young age, my dad was my rock. I excitedly and patiently waited for him to pick me up, in his small blue Datsun. I loved that car with the second-hand and man-made sunroof that needed clear glue to prevent leaking. He would let me shift the gears as he drove. To me, he was the real deal dad; yet, I was told that I should count my blessings that I had other men in my life to care for me. I was not held, comforted, nor told, "I am sorry," by anyone. It was only until writing this book, and my wife forcing me to dive deep into myself, that I realized I still held that pain inside. It was tucked away in isolation, but still visible in my actions. My dad never apologized for his role in giving me up and terminating his parental rights, no explanation at all. Imagine as a young boy, having to change your name in the middle of the year, and having to explain why, as a 12-year-old to your friends. It does something to a boy's confidence, identity, and self-awareness. I wondered, who wanted me? What would I tell my children when I grew up? By not fighting for me, my father basically made me feel that I was not deserving or worthy of his last name. And my mother telling me that I should count my blessings, didn't help at all. It made everything worse.

After that school year, I needed a vacation. I flew to LA for the summer to visit my uncle and his family. This was the summer that my uncle at the age of 35 changed from being a whoremonger, alcoholic, and an adulterer to becoming a true man of God. He has been an ordained minister now for over 30 years. When I returned from California, I was hoping for a better school year. My mother had purchased a new car and mentioned buying a new outdoor pool. I'm thinking, so far so good. Shortly thereafter, she made her grand announcement, "I'm pregnant." I immediately responded, "Kill the baby." My mother was 39 and was told that possible fatal complications could occur by her delivering a newborn. Nevertheless, my brother was born on January 23, 1987. He was beautiful and my little brother. Life was great. I was secretly visiting my dad and I had a cool younger brother. Four months later, my step-father was killed in an auto accident. My mother was devastated, but amazingly strong. For the first time, I realized how proud I was to have her as my mother and how gracious it was to see her unbelievable faith. She was a widow with an infant child and a selfish teenager.

My mother had also been taking care of my grandmother, Madea. She had cancer and started to deteriorate. It was terribly hard seeing my strong grandmother this way. She died one year later. My mother again showed her strength. My dad returned to our lives, stronger than before. My parents became best friends again. My father took on the role of a father to my younger brother as his father had done for me. I can definitely say that my dads were both phenomenal men.

In 1987, I began high school at Magnet High. I was popular and part of the, "in crowd." Prior to attending Magnet High, my counselor from Middle Magnet told me that even if I tested into admission at Magnet, I would fail. Not only did I not fail, I graduated with a high GPA. I also worked during high school. My guy friends, The Mustang Auto Crew and I, would drive to Grambling University and gamble on who could get the most college girls' numbers. We also drove to New Orleans for special events like Bayou Classic and Mardi Gras during our senior year. I had a girlfriend in New Orleans that year and it was also the first time I started to drink, especially with my college friends.

2
Choosing Dentistry

"And when he heard that it was Jesus of Nazareth, he began to cry out, and say, Jesus, thou Son of David, have mercy on me."

~Mark 10:47

After graduation, I matriculated to a private college in New Orleans. College was fun. My parents brought me to New Orleans for freshmen week. My friends were mostly upperclassmen. I remembered the first Saturday night my parents left me with them. Nic took me to the "party house." They asked if I wanted a beer. I refused, but peer pressure really does get the best of you. It definitely happened to me. More and more pretty ladies came to the "party house" drinking. I drank and drank throughout that night. It was insane. After that semester and the holidays, I brought my car to school and moved into my new apartment. This is when the party really began.

My sophomore year approached, and I met my now wife. It was her first year at our university. We dated for approximately two years. I pledged in a fraternity that I later completed. I partied, studied, and was promiscuous all throughout my tenure in college. The summer after my sophomore year, I participated in a dental program at Nashville Dental School. I took the Dental Aptitude Test during the program and did well. I was later told that due to my score and my grades, I could apply for early admission. In February of my junior year, I received a call from the assistant dean of the dental school informing me that I was accepted to the first-year dental class for that upcoming fall year. My response was, "So, no matter what I do, I'm good?" She said, "Yes." The party was on. I only went to classes that I needed for dental school like physiology and biochemistry. I stopped going to the others.

I began dental school with the immature mind of a 20-year-old senior, still in undergrad. There were two other major universities in the same town as my dental school where I did most of my hanging out. We were told on the first week by our dean that Fridays were, "Self-reflect Day," and it was considered a rest day. In my eyes as well as my classmates, it was our party day.

The first major party was on the second Friday of the beginning of the school year at one of my classmate's apartment at the Towers. The Towers was a high-rise apartment complex for students, faculty, and others. She had a couple of gallons of E&J brandy, my old drink. My thoughts were to pour as much of the E&J into my glass since it was free. Drunk, I ran into her apartment wall, head first. I was later found by my friends asleep, in my Mustang, with the windows down while it was raining. They took me back upstairs, but I somehow lost them and eventually woke up hours later on the fifth floor in the hallway of the towers. The rest of the school year was a blur.

My second year approached, and I prepared myself for the most important class, Fixed Prosthodontics. This class was rumored to purposely fail five or more students each year, but I have never failed so I didn't worry. This class was one year long and had to be completed to enter your third year as well as clinicals. There was one project that took the length of the year to complete and was 50% of your grade. In December 1996, I was part of the top 10% of the class that was ahead of the project. I turned the project in for the holidays, I returned in January after the holidays and my project was stolen. I had to start all over. On the last Friday that the project was due for completion, my project was not completed. I knew I failed. I got completely drunk that night. I drove downtown Nashville, ran onto the sidewalk, and hit a huge flower pot. Fortunately, my friends saw me at the light and convinced the police officer to let me go home with them. I risked a DUI, endangering my life and the lives of others because I was ill-equipped in handling the possibility of failure. I ended up completing the project and moving forward. I continued to party hard with my friends, and neighboring college students throughout my tenure in Dental School. I graduated from Dental school in May of 1998. My mother also remarried that day during my graduation party. It was a day of celebration.

After graduation, I returned to Chicago where I had spent many summers as a child when my parents were together. I grew up in Chicago during the summers with my grandmother, Grandmother D, and my fathers' siblings. I was waiting to take the Southern Regional Testing Agency, (SERTA), a dental licensing test which was administered in Memphis. While in Chicago, I hung out with friends and interned at a local dental office. I took the test in November 1998 and received my passing notification letter that December. I immediately moved to Atlanta in January and stayed with my older cousin, John. My first job was with a corporate dental office. I was on a six-month contract. During that period, I began to fall in love with Atlanta's hot club life and beautiful women.

I realized that I was not challenged at the corporate dental practice and rejected the renewal of my contract. I began to work at a dental office in downtown Atlanta. My two employers introduced themselves to me while sipping cognac and being paraded by exotic dancers at an Atlanta Gentlemen's club. They noticed me wearing scrubs, and immediately asked me about my occupation. They bought dances and drinks for me while informing me that they were dentists and needed a new associate. I worked for them from 1999 to 2003. Financially, they took advantage of my inexperience; however, they taught me how to become a skillful dentist as well as an entrepreneur.

3
Becoming a C-Alcoholic

"And straightway the father of the child cried out, and said with tears, Lord, I believe; help thou mine unbelief."

Mark 9:24

In 2000, I was in a terrible accident. It was Memorial Day weekend and my friend, Vic, came to visit. I picked Vic up from the airport around noon and partied all night drinking/clubbing. I finished drinking at 3:00 AM but did not leave the club until 5:00 AM. On the way home, I fell asleep at the wheel near my house and ran head on into a street light pole. My blood alcohol content was .02. There were not any legal consequences, but medically, we had a few complications. Vic fractured his jaw and I fractured my hip. I recovered in four months and still clubbed after my second month of recovery. I would club walking on crutches.

After I healed, I became the life of the party and very known in the club scene. I began to work for my classmate, Dr. Wilkins, as well as the downtown dental office. By 2003, life was getting out of control. I started traveling to Brazil, Costa Rica, Dominican Republic, and Mexico. I even had an incident where I was robbed at gunpoint at my home. My money was increasing and my will to do it my way began to really develop. I had the new house, the Escalade, the motorcycle, and the tab that accompanied it. I purchased an SL500 Mercedes. My flame truly got hotter.

My first DUI was in the Mercedes in 2003. I went to this luxury hotel for happy hour with a beautiful Canadian girl. We left the hotel after several drinks to go to another bar. After paying the toll on GA 400, I sped off and was pulled over for speeding. I was charged with a DUI and my date left in my car. I was fined but received no jail time. I became more and more reckless. I purchased my dental practice in January 2004. As a gift to myself, I upgraded to a 2005 SL600 V12 Mercedes and a new Escalade. I become loose with my money and started making bad decisions. I would fly women into Atlanta. I hung out with ball players, entertainers, and exotic dancers. I was having the time of my life.

In 2005, I purchased an $800,000 house. I was extremely humbled because I never thought that I could afford such a home as well as secure bank financing. Life seemed amazing. I was introduced to Mario, a guy big on the social scene. Socially, I would party with him and his female friends. On a few occasions, I would call in Dr. Smith to work my office. He partied, too.

In May 2005, I took a young lady out for her birthday. We started at Fogo De Chao and drunk several Caipirinhas, a Brazilian sugar cane drink. We left to go to Shooters Alley, a Gentlemen's club, for more drinks. Influenced by the environment, I took my first and last ecstasy pill. The young lady and I left Shooters and attempted Strokers, another Gentlemen's club, but it was closed. I had plenty to drink. For years, I lied about who drove that night. I had to make my statement convincing to myself to be able to convince the judge. It did not work. We drove onto Highway 78 and my friend needed to pull over to vomit. We parked on the side of the road for over an hour. The police noticed us and charged me with a DUI. I plead guilty in early 2006 of DUI and was mandated to a court DUI program and sentenced to 30-day work release program. This program entailed me working during the day and sleeping in jail at night. I stopped drinking and partying after the 30 days. My life seemed to be getting back on track until December 2006. I received terrible news. I received a call from Mario and his girls. I relapsed. I knew that I was going out of town that week and would not be screened until the following Thursday. I partied that Friday and was screened the following Wednesday. I failed my drug/alcohol screen. The charging Judge was furious and sentenced me to a weekend in jail. He ordered me to return to court with my attorney. February 2007, he sentenced me to a rehab facility and ordered me to report both DUI's to the board of dentistry. I had to inform my brother and parents of my addictions. They were very supportive. During that time, my younger brother, a college student, was murdered. He was 20. That nearly destroyed me. I went back to work at the end of May and was arrested in my office for probation violation. I had to serve 40 days. I went back to work in August. I received a letter from the board requesting me to complete a 96-hour evaluation at Ridgeview. It was determined by Ridgeview that I was an impaired professional and needed a 90-day intake program. My dental license was suspended. Through 2008, I had several associate dentists working for my office. The last dentist destroyed my office by not showing up on time or at all and completing horrible dental work. I had the impression that he was going to purchase the office, but because of his credit and poor financial history, he could not. The office numbers greatly decreased; however, God still showed me mercy and favor. It was nothing but God's grace that allowed me to keep that practice open to be sold. I sold my practice in November 2008. I never thought that the office could withstand that long without me there.

After completing my intakes at the treatment center and until now, I have had to continue being monitored and attend AA meetings. These meetings consisted of middle-aged people discussing their family issues singing the familiar song of being depressed and binge drinking. I felt lost and misunderstood. I would be ridiculed, by them, if I began to discuss how I did not have a desire to drink, but more so a desire to go to a strip club. Still mentioning my stronger urges for the strip club rather than alcohol, I was told that I had not owned up to my disease in alcoholism. In fact, I totally understood my desire to get drunk once I was at the strip club or bars with the opposite sex. I realized that my lustful thoughts for the sensual lifestyle was my true addiction. But I did not know how to discuss it and truly get the help from a program such as AA. If I shared my views that I am not an Alcoholic in the premise of the, "traditional definition," of a severe alcoholic, I would be scorned by the masses.

My mission became to adequately define my addiction, so that I could help my circumstance. This became my challenge, and as I pondered through my thoughts and actions, I realized that my alcohol addiction was not the root of my problem. My brain enjoyed the excitement of the music, the smoking and fast women in specific environments. I realized that I had to truly focus and learn tools to enable me to say no to that red man sitting on my shoulder, picking at me to stop at that Gentleman's club for the free open buffet. Was the food calling me or was it the excitement and attention that clouded me as I walked through the doors of those establishments? It was then that I began to understand that there are stages, not just in alcoholism, but in all addictions. I wanted to truly understand so I could understand my behaviors and choices. In this process, I learned that I am what I have defined as a, "C- Alcoholic." With this understanding, I begin my healing process.

4

The Addict's Alphabet

"What has been will be again, what has been done will be done again; there is nothing new under the sun."

~Ecclesiastes 1:9

As I started my journey to understand my addiction, I began to see similarities in the different types of alcoholics and the different types of students I encountered in high school and college. As I attempted to understand my own addiction and behavior, I knew I was not like many of the people I met in Alcoholics Anonymous (AA). I identified different levels of addiction. More importantly, in listening to the different stories and experiences, I realized everyone's story and struggles are not the same. There are varying roots or underlying issues that lead to alcoholism. I was no different. My addiction was not merely the love of and uncontrolled intake of alcohol; it was the environment, attention, and control I was addicted to. My work and healing had to target the root because the alcoholism was just an adjective of it.

Let's consider different performing levels of students. In high school, the, "C student" perhaps does not necessarily feel they have an academic issue because they pass with a C, as compared to the, "F student" who failed and must repeat the course. "C students" may not see any issues with their status as they are still passing; however, they cannot get a scholarship and find it harder to be admitted to a college or university of their choice. So, are they really doing good? Some people can live an average C lifestyle for life and be great. In comparison to a "C- Alcoholic," he/she too can be hard to see as failing or having a problem.

An, "A Alcoholic" would be considered a person who daily drinks a glass of wine or bottle of beer to relax at home. As they are not considered an alcoholic, they still need to have a substance to help them relax. This would cause a reaction from the addiction world. Nevertheless, that one glass is all that they need. Same would be for the "A student." They may need tutoring once or twice, a little help here or there, but they ultimately are doing well and achieving high. No problems, right?

The, "F Alcoholic,"" is the, "paper bag drunk." He/she must drink throughout the day, hiding drinks. He knows that he is a drunk and so do others. He is white but looks black because his liver is gone. He has issues. He is an "Alcoholic."

I am a "C- Alcoholic." The "C- Alcoholic" is a social drinker and does not, initially believe he has an issue as he compares himself to the, "F Alcoholic." He has to go through many tribulations and sometimes several, before he can recognize his problem. He does not think about drinking all day. He drinks when he is out with friends. He is the life of the party. But his problem is that when he is in certain desired scenes, he does not want to just drink one cocktail. He has a high tolerance and because of it, he does not get a quick buzz and appears sober until he has had six or more drinks. There exists no middle for him in this element. Occasionally, he may mask his drinking behaviors and drink one or two cocktails in a slower environment, (dinner with his wife or his mother's birthday dinner) and because of his trickery, his abusive drinking is easily overlooked and denied.

What about the AA scene? The thoughts from the elders in AA is that you are either an alcoholic or not. Needless to say, in Alcoholics Anonymous, there exist different types of alcoholics or alcohol abusers. These types are as followed; The first DUI offender mandated by the court; the "Jekyll and Hyde" drinker who causes issues when drinking; the "All Day" drinker who has to drink, daily. Because of the differences and the thoughts of the elder AA members, the C- Alcoholic is looked over. He dares not say that he could be in a room with alcohol without wanting a drink. If so and as mentioned earlier, he would be scorned as the true drinkers would rise up and call "BS." This scares off the "C- Alcoholic," and frustrates him as he truly is not, yet, dependent on alcohol. He still has control to say no and may not, still, see his issue. If not helped, it is possible that he may eventually become an "F Alcoholic."

Whether you are reading this book for yourself or to better understand someone you love, let's explore the characteristics of these types of alcoholics. I believe these traits or characteristics are conducive to any addiction. My prayer is that you will be able to better identify these behaviors in yourself or a loved one. It's with understanding and clarity that we can begin to heal and change, with God's help. On the next few pages, I have provided a character sketch of the different types of alcoholics, including their characteristics, consumption levels, and values. As you read, see if you can identify yourself or family member. Feel free to use the suffix "holic" to any addiction that you may think is consuming you...sex, shopping, work, or reality tv.

"A- Alcoholic"- Relaxing Drinker

Characteristics
- Does not try to get drunk; will not get drunk; social drinker
- No mood changes once a glass of alcohol is consumed
- Can become dependent on the feel of a daily drink; this is not an alcoholic

Consumption
- Drink a glass of wine daily for the "feel," drinks to relax (1-2 drinks)
- Has control on the amount of intake

Values
- No legal, family, or medical issues

"B- Alcoholic"- Alcohol Abuser

Characteristics
- Has control enough to not drink as needed; Not considered alcoholic
- Can get drunk, as opposed to "A-" but can still stop
- Does not isolate to get drunk

Consumption
- Drinks heavily w/friends or socially
- Light and/or heavy drinking; can moderate his drinking
- 2+ drinks; experimental drinking

Values
- No legal, family, or medical issues

"C- Alcoholic"- The Forgotten Alcoholic/Early Stage Alcoholic

Characteristics
<ul><li>In moment of drinking, does not have control of his drinking</li><li>Compares himself to the "F Alcoholic"</li><li>In denial, does not acknowledge alcoholism; confident in sobriety</li><li>Difficult to diagnose; Everyone protects him/her</li></ul>
Consumption
<ul><li>Drinking is controlled by his environment; possible poisoning</li><li>Early Alcoholic Abuser, social drinker; begins to blackout,</li><li>No isolation; high/increased tolerance level (*key issue</li><li>Does not drink daily nor crave alcohol</li></ul>

Continued the next page

Values
- Possibility of values challenged; Legal Issue-Inhibition is different
- May or may not have legal/family/medical issues (issues become possible)
    - Ex: Does not remember 1-night stands

"D Alcoholic" - Moderate Stage Alcoholic

Characteristics
- Consistent blackouts- several (multiple); High Tolerance and starts to isolate
- Has given up trying to stop (middle class alcoholic)
- Often exhibited in families and learned behavior

Consumption
- Moderate alcoholic, social drinker
- Drinks heavily; takes 4-5 drinks to get person drunk, as opposed to 1 or 2

Values
- Legal/family/medical issues
- Common Medical Issues: Heart Failure; Alcoholic Hepatitis, Cancer, Chronic Bronchitis

"F Alcoholic" – End stage of Alcoholism

Characteristics
- Extremely high-tolerance
- Needs detox; service drinking by continuing
- All characteristics of "C- "and "D" Alcoholic

Consumption
- Consumption daily
- Drinks heavily and constantly

Values
- Exhibits both physical and mental health issues
- Body detoxification- liver issues
- Liver destroyed medical, physical, mental issues

I represented the characteristic and denial of a "C- alcoholic" in my early rehabilitated years. On my first DUI, and in the beginning of this entire process, a Rehab representative asked me if I was going to be able to drink again. Unknowing, I said, yes, I will be able to drink again. I did not think that I had an issue as all of my friends drank similar to me. Maybe I was an alcoholic or maybe not, all I know is that alcohol had gotten in my way. Fortunately, I was forced to do a 90-day inpatient program. It was really a country club for the wealthy whites with a sprinkle or two of black individuals. It forced me to look at myself. In the beginning of rehab, I blamed everyone but me. I would say that I got a DUI only because I was pulled over being a black man driving an expensive car, and maybe so. Maybe I did get pulled over for being black driving an expensive car, but I got a DUI because I was "drunk" driving it." I have learned to own up to my choices and behaviors. The word "Alcoholic" is difficult to say especially if it is not your primary addiction. Whether I am an alcoholic or not, the fact is that alcohol has caused me unwanted issues, period. I have disposed of any of my comparisons of those around me and have focused on scaling my truth. It has always been about my actions and my relationship with God. I have learned how to be my own critic knowing that mistakes will take place and that it is okay to make them as long as you recognize them, ask for forgiveness, and learn from them. Acknowledge your truth

Evaluate Your Issues and Actions

Now it's time to evaluate yourself, not only within alcoholism, but addiction and life struggles. Is anything out of control in your life? What is inside of you that is causing you to have the repercussions and the impacts on your family, legal, and medical values?

You must take responsibility. Accept what you are doing to help contribute to the root issue or problem. This book is not about "C- Alcoholics." Alcoholism may not be your issue, but it is mine. In all addictions, there are commonalities. We must get to the root and the core issue to own our actions.

5
Surrendering to the Lord

"The grace of God teaches us to say no."
~Titus 2:11-12 NIV

It is written, "For what is a man profited, if he shall gain the whole world, and lose his own soul? or what shall a man give in exchange for his soul?" (Matt 16:26 KJV) I have learned that God only puts on you as much as you can bear. The Bible states, "I can do all things through Christ, who strengthens me." (Phil 4:13) I could have lost it all, but now I truly see that He has always been there for me. I am here at this place in my life and it's a blessing. It is a blessing that I have a chance to get my life back, which includes my health, my soul, my finances, my self- respect, and mostly, my relationship with my God.

God provided me with the financial means to be here. The temptation of alcohol or sexual dependency will never go away, but God will give me the strength to resist thru his Word. I feel that I am becoming more equipped to live with it. The Bible, as well as my self-confrontation, is providing me with the necessary tools to continually help me fight these demonic sensations of my flesh. Each is making me accountable. I am now seeking a life with Godly problems and Godly results that are resolved through Godly decisions.

"Trust in the lord with all your heart; and lean not to your own understanding, in all your ways acknowledge Him and he will make your path straight." (Proverbs 3:5)

6
Values

Willing to lose, love it more.
"Learn on sense what is vital... and of real value."
~Jentezen Franklin

Values
Family
Finance
Freedom
God
Health

Dan Mager, MSW wrote in Psychology Today, that, "Personal values provide an internal compass that points the way to what an individual identifies as positive, healthy, beneficial, valuable, useful, desirable, and constructive." I agree with Mr. Mager that my life became more satisfying and I found myself content when I realigned to my values, respecting, and honoring them with my choices/actions. Your integrity is essentially the level to which your actions align with your values. I believe five values are central and core to all people: Education, Finance, Family, Spiritual, and Health.

"Active addiction usually takes people away, often light-years away, from their values." (Mager, 2018) In the right environment to get what I wanted, I started very subtly to move away from my values, and over time my choices were blatantly more satisfying which led to my addiction.

Patrick writes in Spiritualriver.com, "... that values help to define our approach to recovery..." Let's consider these values and how they might have changed based on our behavior. Since values are whatever we hold to be good, many people value health, family, and/or money.

I believe a person's tolerance level plays a key role in a person's addiction, whether it be alcohol, drugs, sex, or pornography. According to DrugAbuse.com, there are three main types of tolerance:

Acute, or short-term, tolerance is caused by repeated exposure over a relatively short period of time.

Chronic, or long-term, tolerance develops when an individual's body adapts to constant exposure over weeks or months; building up chronic tolerances

Learned tolerance may result from frequent exposure; Experimental studies have shown that drinkers can compensate for the effects of alcohol on their coordination when they practice a task repeatedly while under the influence (Vogel-Sprott, M.,1997).

Tolerance refers to a decrease in brain sensitivity to alcohol following long-term exposure – during tolerance, there is reduction in the intensity of the effect of alcohol/ drugs over the course of repeated use. Amount of alcohol increases to get the same effect. To overcome my high tolerance, I looked to the Lord on how to deal with my tolerance and appeal of the sin of alcohol. In The Secrets of Self-Control daily devotions, Jentezen Franklin says, "Don't look for God to nullify the appeal of sin; ask him for the power to overcome its appeal." And so, I ask you…What are you going to do when that specific temptation comes around? Through God's grace and mercy, you are equipped to resist.

I have realized by reading the Bible on several occasions, that the Word is a history book of the Israelites. However, it's also a guide on how to live. It has characters that have done everything, and you can imitate whatever character you want. The ultimate goal is to become more and more like Jesus every day.

7

Dealing with Self
(Self- Control)

"No temptation has overtaken you except what is common to mankind. And God is faithful; he will not let you be tempted beyond what you can bear. But when you are tempted, he will also provide a way out so that you can endure it."

~ I Cor 10:13

I had to learn to be truthful with myself, focusing on changing my behavior, and I want you to do the same. The goal is to evaluate yourself, to identify your root issue, and how your issues have affected the five values (in the previous chapter) in your life. Addiction is not just relative to alcoholism; too much of anything is not good for you. Identify, name, and point to your "-holic" so you can take control of it, and take your life back, in Jesus Name.

"Let the spirit direct your lives." (Galatians 5:16 GNT) It is easier to give in to sin than to say no. The devil is cunning and conceiving, "Let the spirit direct your lives and you will not satisfy the desires of the human nature." Notice it did not say that you won't have the desires. Being spirit filled does not mean that you won't have the desires, you are just equipped to not satisfy them. This was last because I had to realize that the only way for me to leave my addiction was to, "pick up my cross and die daily."

In my "C-Alcoholic" addiction, I blacked out and didn't remember entire nights. I had no idea what I did. I had value issues:

1. **Freedom**- Began to have legal issues

2. **Family**- Inappropriate behavior with other women

3. **Finance**- Risked my career getting DUI's; court and rehab costs

4. **God**- Constant Sin

5. **Health-** Weight gain, sleep disorder, hypertension

God knows that we are going to sin, but He wants us to be devoted to Him. Jesus answered and said unto them, "Ye do err, not knowing the scriptures, nor the power of God." (Matt 22:29)

You tell yourself in the morning that you won't do "it" again because of how you felt when you woke up. However, you find yourself doing that same sin the following day/week. This makes sense because John 8:34 states, "Everyone who sins, is a slave to sin."

Tell God your specific problems and ask God to deliver you from it according to Romans 14:4 NLT, "With the Lord's help, you will stand." Understand that you try to stop and may fail while trying. If you feel as if you can't stop or help yourself, please know that this is a common misconception. Paul says in 2 Corinthians 4:9 JLB, "We get knocked down, but we get up again and keep going." Don't focus on past failures as it will lead to repeating them. When you realize doing it your way and not God's way, does not work, it is a defining moment and victory. (Romans 14:9)

Titus 2:11-12 NIV declares, "The grace of God teaches us to say no." Talk back to your feelings when you find yourself saying things like:

- I have to have this drink
- I don't feel like getting up
- I don't feel like going to church
- I need to go to the strip club

Instead:

- Don't give your feelings so much power
- Tell your feelings, "No"
- Declare, God gives you the power to resist through His Word

Philippians 4:13 says, "I can do all things, through Christ who strengthens me." Renew your mind to God's Word. My mother would tell me when I was a kid, "Boy, don't let the devil make a fool out of you." I say the same to you. You have to transform your mind; you have to fill your mind with the promises of God. I Corinthians 10:13 NIV says, "When you are tempted, He will always provide a way out so that you can stand up under it." Amen! You can try to change your behavior yourself, but ultimately you set yourself up for failure. "Jesus said unto him, if thou canst believe, all things are possible to him that believeth." (Mark 9:23)

The Bible tells us to, "Share each other's burden." (Galatians 6:2) Don't be embarrassed about your issues. If you did it, you did it. Claim it. If I did whatever, I did it because I wanted to. Stop getting angry at people who gossip about what you did. You did it. By acknowledgment of "it," you become free and you release its power over you, according to Ephesians 4:27 GNT, "Don't give the devil a chance."

Avoid situations that you know are going to cause temptation in your life. If you are on a diet and you love cheesecake, why would you go to the Cheesecake Factory. You would be hurting yourself. 1 Corinthians 15:33 NIV says, "Bad company corrupts good character." Think about what you need to avoid. A relationship, a certain club, certain magazines, people/places/things. Literally, stand on your Bible and tell the Lord, "I'm not strong enough to resist this temptation by myself. Help me Lord!" Tell Him the exact temptation and I promise you, He will! (Psalms 40:1-3 CRV)

My Prayer

I patiently waited for you Lord to hear my prayer, you listened and pulled me up from a lonely pit full of mud and mire. You let me stand on a rock with my feet firm. Many will see this, and they will honor and trust you, the Lord God.

Call to Action

1. I challenge you to read a Scripture every day. Start with, "A man's temptation is due to the pull of his own desires which greatly affects him." (James 1:4) Pounder on the Scripture and write what it means, applying to your life. You can summarize this scripture as, "Accept responsibility of your actions, your sins. Admit your problem and issues. You, and you alone must see that you have a "problem." I had to realize that it takes more drinks for me to get drunk due to my tolerance. So, I started telling myself, "No, No more. There are consequences to my actions." I learned to accept responsibility through this Scripture. That is when God began to do a new work in me. Now you summarize in your own words. Then, apply.

_____

_____

_____

2. Consider making a list of the actions that you need to change, say 'No' to, or deny yourself. Think about how your values have been affected by these actions. Evaluate how your life is going to change as you say No and deny your root or issue.

_____

_____

_____

_____

_____

_____

_____

_____

_____

_____

_____

_____

8

Lessons and Tools

"Now unto him that is able to do exceeding abundantly above all that we ask or think, according to the power that worketh in us,"

~Ephesians 3:20

The most important lesson I learned in overcoming my addiction and how to change, was the power in praying and reading Scripture daily. Reading Scripture daily holds me accountable and sustains me. My change occurred through His Word, and I believe it is the same for you too. The only thing that I can do, is to do what I am supposed to be doing... praying unceasingly.

I also believe that God uses heat to refine us and to show His reflection in us. The Bible often uses the imagery of gold being refined as a picture of what He chooses to use in our lives. I'd like to consider this as it relates to us, and our addictions.

When gold is extracted from the earth, it does not look like gold in a jewelry store and it is not always recognizable due to impurities and an affected appearance. But an ugly lump of gold has huge potential and hidden beauty. I believe how gold is found, represents us. The sacrifice of God's Son to reconcile us back to relationship with Him shows just how much God loves and values us -- even while we lose sight of Him and our values. I believe God sees us full of potential and He is the refiner.

God loves us too much to leave us as we are because our impure selves cannot reflect clearly all of who He is, and our fullest joy is realized in the growing brilliance of our reflection of Him in our lives. The refining process is hot applying force to remove the impurities from the surface. As the impurities rise, they are removed and the heat increases, continuing repeatedly until the gold is pure. The refiner knows the gold is pure when he looks into the gold and sees his clear reflection. And that my friend, is God refining us until He can see Himself in our image.

Our lives are a process of God applying heat and exposing our weaknesses, our struggles; our addictions. Heat is hot and uncomfortable, but if we submit to the heat process, we transform into His likeness, day by day, month after month. The process ends when we meet Jesus face to face, and He looks into our faces and sees His clear reflection. Amen! Let's submit to and trust God's process. In the next section I am going to share some Tools and Keys to Success for the journey.

Tools

Find someone who will check on you, pray with you and encourage you in areas where you want and need more self-control. "For two people can resist an attack that would defeat one person alone." (Ecclesiastes 4:12)

List 3-4 people you can ask to check on and encourage you.

_____

_____

_____

_____

_____

Suggestions for accountability partner:

1. Same gender
2. Someone you can depend on that will follow through on helping you, keeping you accountable.
3. Someone who is faithful and will keep your secrets.

List 3-4 people who you can ask to be your accountability partner.

_____

_____

_____

_____

_____

Keys to Success

1. Realize that you can fail
2. Don't put too much pressure on yourself
3. Claim whatever you love. Be specific to God
4. Pray each morning and stay in your Word
5. Anoint my head with oil and recite. ~Psalms 23
6. Made amends to those I love
7. Shared my shortcomings with family, friends, and others
8. Stop being ashamed
9. Opened up
10. Be more accountable
11. List verses recite I can do all things through Christ
12. Start loving God more than I love myself

Bet on Yourself

In the years of Jesus, the cross was not this shiny, smooth, piece of jewelry that we wear on our neck. The cross represented wrongdoings and shameful acts. It meant that you were ridiculed and have done evil. It was punishment and your death sentence. Something has to die in you each day someone angers you. You must kill that evil response that you were about to unleash: 1) Someone cut you off while driving and your reaction; 2) Your boss screams at you for something that you did not do. You have to die daily.

We say, I am not good enough to have God's spirit in my life. Once I get my act together, then I am going to let the Holy Spirit control my life. God does not say, "Get your act together and then I will help you." He says, "Let my Holy Spirit control you while you are still struggling with the problem. I will help you change." His promise is extremely important. You shouldn't say, "Let me get well first and then I will go see the doctor." You need Christ in your life now to help you change. God wants the glory.

The Burning Flame Theory

Importantly, and as slightly described earlier, I have to emphasize what truly saved my life which is what I call, "The Burning Flame Theory." To get the glory, God will allow you to go through your "Burning Flame" like precious metals, and like precious metals, God uses the "Burning Flame" to remove all of your impurities and forms you into His desired image, so when He takes you out of the "Burning Flame," He can polish you up and see His image within you. But like all precious metals, sometimes, it will get a little dusty, but the true blessing is that it has already been shaped and needs, only, a good, old-fashioned, spit shine. He is able and how I know is, as a tear trickles down my face writing this, is because He has done immeasurable mercies for me before and I am still here able to praise Him. He is my Lord and Savior, and I love Him. In Jesus name, Amen!

Sources

Alcohol Facts and Statistics. (n.d.). Retrieved from
https://www.niaaa.nih.gov/alcohol-health/overview-alcohol-consumption/alcohol-facts-and-statistics

Mager, D. (2017, July 27). Values Can Be a Conduit to Recovery. Retrieved from
https://www.psychologytoday.com/us/blog/some-assembly-required/201707/values-can-be-conduit-recovery

What Is Process Addiction & Types of Addictive Behaviors? (n.d.). Retrieved from
https://americanaddictioncenters.org/behavioral-addictions/#stats

About the Author

Dr. S. Collins was born in Shreveport, LA and was later adopted by his mother's husband, who's now deceased. His younger, only brother was murdered at the age of 20 changing his life forever. Dr. Collins majored in chemistry at a renown HBCU. He went on to pursue his doctorate degree from Meharry Medical College School of Dentistry and is a fellow at the International Academy of Dental Implantology. Dr. Collins has been a member of the National Dental Association (NDA) and the Student Competition for Advancing Dental Research & Application (SCADA). He is a proud member of an African American Fraternity. He has practiced dentistry for over 20 years and grew his expertise by self-starting two thriving practices.

Dr. Collins met and dated his wife while they were undergraduate students. Although both were too young to commit at that time, they reconnected later in life. Today, they are happily married with two beautiful children. He and his family are active in their church, participating in weekly worship, Sunday School and Bible Study. Dr. Collins is a faithful believer in Jesus Christ and today he shares his testimony with you and the world.

www.ingramcontent.com/pod-product-compliance
Lightning Source LLC
Chambersburg PA
CBHW031424290426
44110CB00011B/520